Rescuing the Storm

By

CL Bledsoe

ISBN: 978-93-6354-198-6

First Edition: 2026
Rs. 200/-

Cyberwit.net
HIG 45 Kaushambi Kunj, Kalindipuram
Allahabad - 211011 (U.P.) India
http://www.cyberwit.net
Tel: +(91) 9415091004
E-mail: info@cyberwit.net

Printed at Repro India Limited.

The poems in this collection originally appeared in the following publications:

The Alembic, Autumn Sky Poetry Daily, Bipolar Poetry, Clockwise Cat, The Dead Mule School of Southern Literature, Does It Have Pockets?, Dog Water, Door is a Jar, Eunoia Review, La Rotonde Review, Lothlorien Poetry Journal, Louisiana Literature: A Review of Literature and the Humanities, MoonLit Getaway, Right Hand Pointing, Slant, Stone Poetry Quarterly, table//FEAST Literary Magazine, 13 Myna Birds and BlazeVOX.

Contents

I was almost stardust myself

after a line by Christina Borgoyn

It never ends, that's what they say.
Or it ends but it's like a movie
you can start over on a fast-food-
and-extra-fries kind of day. The credits
roll and no one else seems worried.
So much is left to chance. The trajectory
of the bullet through the dark room
at night. The sound of the whippoorwill
calling Poor Will. What did he ever do?
After a while, willpower drops like a bottle
of juice on the not-that-clean floor. I've had
enough but I get distracted so easily. Now,
I'm going to get ants. The lights are on.
The lights are off. I had a shot
at the pearly gates, but their teeth
just shined too bright.

I Have Decided to Rescue the Storm,

after an apocryphal line by Matisse

I have decided to rescue the storm,
the fallen branches of my life. I am swept
away by my own intentions and so little
else. The skies, clear in morning. Mud
drying along the road. Fire that only
burns the air and doesn't warm.
I'd like to find an explosion
of blackbirds fleeing the scene,
and take it home for a nice dessert.
But not everyone is comfortable
with destruction. The truth
of adulthood is that even our tragedies
are commonplace. But the bank
owns so much. All around me
is middle management calling
its own name. Clean pants and see-through
eyes. They're so pretty and have such
nice things. My couch is older than my
teeth. My carpet is worn floor.
It's not enough to lie down
in the evenings; I need to hear someone
else's dreams come morning.

The Yips

after a line by Fitzgerald

It takes two to make an accident.
One to hold the map, the other
to work the radio. Someone napping
in the back seat and dreaming
of the World Series. I made a detour
for my good intentions. It was you
and me, the ants, a tree with our initials
carved in at the only rest stop with clean
toilets on the East Coast. Sobering up
at the gas station. Funyuns and Beef jerky.
Buying scratch offs and forgetting quarters.
I stole the keys. Drove us back to your
place. Night blindness and pedestrians.
It meant so much to get it right.
Inside, it was all Hoarders on A&E.
Lingerie the mice had gotten into.
You made me stand outside the door while
you tried to find the couch. You don't
understand. I have to get home
tonight. You have no ambition beyond
the flowers dying on your coffee table.

Thunderstorm

Back in the days when I was a thunderstorm,
there was brief lightning after every
utterance. I fell and fell, water carpeting
my apartment, making all the boards curl.
Nothing could last without turning
into ruin. I felt no sun burning
through the haze. No warmth except
in my rain. Children blinked to see
me. The old just shook their heads
from their porches. Who would take the time
to run through my onslaught in the hopes
of finding warmth inside? It's only water
in there, the odd fish I've carried with me
since childhood. I waited for overcast
days when I could lie in bed and stay
out of the air. The wind was my only friend.
I dreamed of someday drying out, finding
someone else to fall on.

Fat Old Sun

Fat old sun, an orange beset
by ants. They'll never get it home
no matter how pitifully the queen
yelps. The day is falling
toward night and I can't find
myself. I've looked everywhere.
The drip of morning, coalescing
into alchemy, wasn't particularly
promising. But all that's gone, now.
I've never seen anything like you
and I don't want to again. Tell me
my name, and I'll let it fall, Frère
Jacques all over the windowpane.
A patina of meaning somewhere
outside. Or so they say. All I ever
saw was skint knees and shame.
I'm out of chocolate, which is better
in most ways than hope. Lie
in my bed a little while. Just until
I fall asleep. Then you can rob
me blind.

The Mortician's Friendly Smile

How much of our lives is spent
convincing the mortician we aren't
rotting? Scented soaps to hide
the smell. Hard scrubs to pick off dead
skin. What is a whistle for if not
to confuse the predators? When I see
a coffin in the street,
I can't help but stare. When the dogs
come, I've got some raw meat in
a baggie in my pocket to distract
them. I'll toss it one way and run
the other. If that doesn't work,
there are always tummy tickles.
Or succumbing to the teeth. How
many of our words are just loud
air to frighten away the void. It
doesn't like awkward silences, weird
comments, weeping in darkness,
though that's what it often sees.
Sometimes, I take the lettuce into
my hands and tear it with my teeth
just to remind myself what it feels
like to be alive. If any salad is reading
this, I know you can never forgive me.
It's a flaw in our makeup that we've
got to die, we've got to kill in order
to live, we've got to live in order to die.

Almost

They threw me in a box, waited
till 5 a.m. when I was too sleepy
to argue, nailed a lid on and spent
the next three days knocking
and asking if I'd seen the remote.
I wrote my life story in blood
on the inside of the lid. Well, it
was a red pen I had in my pocket.
But still, it was a nice effect.
Birth, the early years I don't recall
which must mean they were better.
A montage of cheeses I'd never
tasted before. Peanut butter combined
with various things. Someone
who once said my name and meant it.
On the third day, they let me out
to use the bathroom. There was so
much color everywhere. The majestic
brown of the grave. The warm pink
of the worms. The sky was a vibrant gray
above the parking lot. I couldn't help
but be thankful.

My Mistakes

A group of my mistakes cornered me
in a park. I was only there to walk other
people's dogs. One wore a beanie and one
wore a cap. The rest had lush hair and hate
on their lips. They introduced themselves
curtly. The beanie was the first woman
I'd ever loved. The hat was the second.
"I didn't mean it," I said, which was patently
a lie. I'd meant every word. "It was the best
I could do at the time." That might've
been true. The one with the beanie shoved
me over, and the one with the lushest hair
had crawled behind me on all fours so I fell
over him. I sprawled in the dirt. "Just let
me do you again," I pleaded. "I'll say
I'm sorry. I'll be more considerate. I won't
say the thing I said." "It's too late,"
the one with the beanie said. "You've ruined
it all." "I know," I said. "I should've never
left the apartment." The one with a shaved
head raised his hand. There were so many,
it was easy to lose track.

Pockets

There's a kind of dust that's the ghost
of water. I slip some into my pocket
to slake my hunger. I've got many walls
to cross in the coming months, heating
in the wind. All those yesterdays
whittled down into dust. Do I remember
their faces? My mother's. My brother's.
This woman who was supposed to be
my life or this one? My pockets are full
of death and dust and my shoes are wearing
out. The wind complains about how
I clutter the landscape. I just want
to be right, one time. I want to be
where I belong.

Red Car

There is a red car. Beside a thick
Eastern white pine. There is a red
car with a donut tire. Music floods
through the walls. It is inescapable.
There are bushes trimmed too short.
Squirrels and crows. A child screams
in the hallway. There is a red car
and a girl turning back with a smile
as she approaches. The boy behind her
says something in Spanish and she
laughs. Cars flow by, the loudest river
that can never be crossed twice. A bike
rack across the road for tourists. Trees
but no deer. An infinite number
of monkeys on TV. There is a red car.
Just enough gas to make it out of town.

River

There's a river between us and a thousand
miles, muddy water and fish you shouldn't
eat. All broken road and swaying bridges.
I'm sorry I wasn't what you wanted. You
weren't either, but neither of us could admit
it. I'll be home when someone dies. I'll
stay long enough to see them disappeared.
Maybe we can lunch and get a room. I'll
bring my backpack. You hit a certain age
and realize nothing ever went right, even
the stuff that did. There's not much longer
to go in this season. Staying home nights
because I don't have to put on pants. It's
warm here and they play the music I like.
I was so desperate for love back then, I
would've followed anyone home.
The difference now is that they lock the door.

The Body

The body wants to be in love,
but the heart says, "Wait.
The sky might turn dark, today,
or never again. The kitchen
is mostly stocked. Why ever
go outside yourself when
there's misery enough in here
for us all?" The secret is telling
your name without hitting
the consonants too hard.
A time you'd rather not mention
nailed onto soap board. The eyes,
impassive as a crossed leg.
You say, "Open, for me,
just once, but never close."

Breath

Nothing is as valuable as breath; bitcoin
won't save the drowning man no matter
what podcasts he listens to. I'm thinking
this as I'm pawing for air in my living room.
I'd rather drown. It hurts to read poetry.
It hurts to watch that new show everyone's
so excited about, the one they'll find problematic
in a month. The problem with good intentions
is the time they waste. Life cannot be quantified
as easily as the preachers want to tell us.
The trick is remembering you're alive
even when you're not.

Press On

A trashcan lined with rage.
No one can trust their neighbors
to water the plants anymore.
A dog whistle. A barking head.
I'm talking about Daylight Savings Time
by years instead of hours.
Should I get stabbed in the back or watch
my enby shot. Should I pretend
there's anything to do but press on?
Let's all post the richest outrage
on social media. You've got jokes. Listen:
No one wants to hear that shit.
I'm trying to hide behind the curtain
but my gut sticks out.
Aside from being the dumbest asses
in captivity, everyone is so fucking
smart. I'm too safe to be
this tired. Imagine. It's my
fault. No, it's their fault. Their
parents. Their school boards.
It's everything just to be right now.

Good Intentions

I left home when the angst threatened
to flood the levee in the back yard.
No one could keep dry in the high winds.
It was me and my best friend loneliness,
waiting for something to happen. It never
did and then it did so fast you couldn't
blink without missing tomorrow. I never
had a plan and I wasn't too good on
the fly, either, buzzing around the room
looking for someone's ears to land on.
I had good intentions which is another
way of saying bend over but don't expect
a second date. It's been so long since I lost
everything, I don't even remember where
to look. They call sometimes, the old hurts,
when I'm watching TV or driving. Remember
that time I did unforgivable things to you, they
say? I didn't mean it. That's fine, I say.
I didn't mean it either. But I did.

How I Discovered Terror

You have to get behind things to see
what really holds them back. The couch
might leap free if it's not tied down.
The dog might eat a cloud if you stop
smearing meat on its face long enough
for it to remember its wings. My father
could terrify me without uttering
a word; he only had to flash me
his aching hands, swollen red, and try
to count out the days since last he'd
smiled with all his teeth. In the other
room, mom couldn't remember how
to open the window. Every time
someone closed the door, she got
excited, thinking this would be
it, but it never opened,
no matter how much she prayed.

A Lonesome Train in the Distance

Trying to tell you something
about my childhood, all you hear
are the rolling hills, cattle lowing
while a train thuds past. Cousins
and aunts gathered to break peas,
shuck corn, lie about whoever isn't
listening. Winters, when snow
finally showed its face, we'd sled
down the ridge to the plain below.
The stock pond sat at its terminus.
We dug for gold in the gravel
hills. But the reason we ran wild
was because no one was chasing
us. I'd stay with Dad while he drank
and told jokes with his drunk friends
and Mom screamed at the dark, at
home. Whatever it was she saw
was why I was afraid to walk alone.
Nothing is owed to us by anyone,
which is something I learned young.
But it would be nice to see it
as you see it, green hills and deep
blue sky that didn't echo with
grief, plain as mud.

My Grief

A bull, snorting
and tearing up
loam in the north
pen. We keep it alone
so it won't hurt
the other cows.

Black hide, plain
as mud. You can smell
it when the breeze shifts.

Offer it blood.
Offer it hay.
Offer it freedom.

My grief smiles.
It is my brother, now.
Come and see, it says.
Come and see.

Stop Trying

Let's pretend history paid attention
instead of falling asleep in its popcorn.
I was old, even when I was young.
That doesn't mean I was ever good
with money. Take me back to next
Tuesday so I can order that sandwich
again. Hot pepper spread. Fancy mustard.
I'm sorry to tell you that this is all
you're ever going to get, so you better
savor the aioli. You can hold out for clean
days. Something to wait for if you can just
last. File the correct requisition form with Time,
but you have to wait until the bank's open
to see the notary. Hold your breath and wish
something happens before the thud.
It's all happened again because you were
too stupid to stop trying.

Swimming

I was swimming with the fishes when a fish stole my watch.
It was a rainy day, which is hard to tell underwater.
I was wearing my best suit, the one made of rubber
that smells like batman.
I wasn't underwater; I was in my bathtub.
This was my hobby, back in the carefree days; swimming
with fish, talking with parrots, generally fucking shit up.
This is what happens when you live alone long enough.
You fill a tub with fish and a room with parrots.
Don't get me started on the burros.
The orange sky of morning. I would tie them to my hands
and feet and pretend I was one of them.
This was all about to change with the new zoning board.
No more slinky giraffes to stand tall with in the back yard.
I'd have to go back to watching football. Who knows
what the tub would be for then.

New Year

A branch rotting in a ditch.
A squirrel fallen from a tree.
I'm so dead, I'm still in the phone book.
I'm having the botflies over for tea.
When you live for one thing, it's hard
to find someone to hang out with
who doesn't spend the hour watching the clock.
I stayed up till 8 and watched fireworks on my phone.
I dreamed about nothing and liked it.
Life is like traffic on 95.
All rush then adding up numbers from license plates.
The stickers are so rarely clever.
If you neglect your house long enough,
your kids will have to clean it.
Unless you don't have kids. Then, you're screwed.

Can't Never Could

The sun came up just to hear
you crow. It didn't have anything
else going on that day. A trail
of red hair halfway down your
back. Eyes green as envy.
Staring at you is like looking
at the sun while the moon picks
my pocket. You gave me two
nickels and I bought a dime.
I was plumb in your arms.
A royal plum. A crooked pot
looking for a lid. You clouded
up and rained all over me. You were
the mayor of worthless,
with a fancy new sash. I put
a colander under the bed. I chased
you like a herd of turtles,
ignoring the eagle floating above.

Parking

Sometimes, not remembering where
you parked is enough. I'm not supposed
to tell you the correct way to pronounce it,
but it rhymes with no. Keys in hand, step
away from the elevator. If a window's open,
beware of crosses. This is not the time
to rest. Strangers throw their hearts at you
as you pass by on the way to 711. The only
reason you're going is because your boss
wanted to talk about his weekend. Maybe
it was on a side street. Maybe you took
the bus. What more can you ask of yourself?
The answer is everything. Listen, no one
cares that you played a good game when
the bullet punches through. Empty your
pockets. You have such wonderful things.
A feather from a common mistake. An un-
exploded clod. A one-size-fits-all coffin
in which to keep your shoes. Peace, still
in its original packaging. Careful,
you think, as it slips through your fingers.

I Am a Ghost

I don't know if it's morning or night, yet,
but they're already in the hall, door pried

off hinges, lights painting the walls.
Their little radio machine beeps. Sometimes,

I like to make it surge like a Theremin.
I saw one at a Sonic Youth show. They

get really excited when I do that, talking
in their little headsets. Their voices are

the mutters of worms, chewing a corpse.
They wave the machine around. They have

a machine that looks for cold spots.
They're very sure of what they'll find,

even though they never find it. Always
when I'm trying to read, to watch TV

on the radio waves. I thought this was
supposed to be my time of peace. Not kids

looking for proof they haven't wasted
it all in vain, that there will be another

chance, floating in the dark, messing with
teenagers and Travel Channel Documentarians.

The Finale of Seem

Someone is talking in the back
of my standup routine. What
they're saying is funnier
than me. The waves are coming
and I don't know how
to surf. No one has wished me
a happy birthday since May.
It's okay. Everything I love
was taken by James Franco. He's
working on two degrees at a time.
A school banned a book written
by its namesake. This is
the greatest lesson they ever taught.
When I hear noises at night, I hope
it's ghosts and not robbers. I'd hate
to have to invite them for tea.
I just won a lawsuit against
the angels. All that wing dander
makes me sneeze on dates.
Something is chewing on my
ceiling. I don't know if it's
a squirrel or a child. Either way,
I can bribe it with peanuts.
If only all problems were so easy
to solve.

The Sun

We waited for the lightning, but it never
came. So, we assumed we were in the clear.
The secret of momentum is to never stop
falling. The knees are the first to go.
Followed by everything else. No one
will applaud no matter how well you stick
the landing. Looking back to that day
that was a parenthesis ruined by your
punctuation. You could never sit still
long enough to catch the air. It will never
be that good again without some body
language to finesse the scene. Now, the day
is teething, which explains the wincing light.
I can never remember the sun's name
until it's set. Then its feelings are already hurt.
The sound of rain is its first betrayal.
Then the fog obscuring the way home.
Who wants to go where they've already
been anyway? At least it hides the sun
with all its pouting.

This Is a Poem About Loss

As in, I can't find my car keys,
so I haven't left the apartment
in a week. It's spring outside
my window, which means
the allergies are in bloom. Children
play into the night. I listen to them
while I read in bed. The world
is changing but my apartment
is the same. When I bring my
child, I spray everything with Lysol
in hopes she won't catch whatever
I've got.

Train whistles

Long mornings listening to cows chew cud
outside my bedroom window. The fence had
been down for years. Dad had settled into
his alcoholism with no intention of fixing it.
I could hear trains whistle down the hill.
I could've jumped on board and ridden
to Memphis at any time, but I was weighted
down by the grief of it all. Nights, witches
scratched the walls outside. Cows moaned
from their wallows in the distance. Coyotes
sang beyond the light. It would've been ideal
if it weren't for the suffering. I tried outpacing
it but never could keep my shoes tied.

Cheese Dip

I'm just doing this for the dough
and the ladies. Gingerbread women
especially appreciated. I just turned
16 yesterday and now it hurts
when I wake up. What a joke, but I'm
the only one laughing. Just let me close
my eyes a little while and listen to your
smile. I'll take the parking ticket gladly.
It takes an eternity to live and about 15
minutes to die. And then we start over
next Tuesday. I sent a love letter
to the world and it was returned postage
due. What about you? Are you ready
to lie down into a new world? We can fade
into each other and only get up to answer
the door. They're just selling heaven,
but we have chips and cheese dip.

The Old Question

Maybe God is real, in the eternal embrace
of a sigh, the digestive tract of a crow
processing French fries. I believe nothing
is anything more than it seems, which is a scream
of frustration from the world that will never
be. I was never cool, even with my
leather jacket. Is God to blame for that?
It all has to do with the lean. I was always
too nervous not to care. If I had the detachment
of God, I could've ruled the world, but wouldn't
have wanted to. But really, it's about
the opposition. The devil is evil so there must
be a force of good. Life is finite so there must
be something ongoing. I never wanted to live
forever, barely wanted to make it through many
a day. So much of it all is about shame.

The Okie Doke of the Soul

Jillian gave me flowers for my birthday,
daisies and pansies. I put them on my patio
so I could sit and enjoy them while
Anna tells me how my father has taken
to pissing in the litter box in the middle
of the night. It's his commentary on
pet ownership. I had to hide my rocking
chair because it's inside furniture, but
it's been outside so long, it doesn't fit
anymore. Due diligence for the HOA,
which will never check again. I'm not
an owner, I'm a renter. When it got warm,
I moved everything back out, the rocking
chair, a table, the flowers on a plastic rug.
My father does whatever anyone tells him.
Then, at night, he finds the packages of
adult diapers and slashes them with a pocket
knife. I remember the first time I flew,
worrying what I'd do without my knife.
I was afraid to check it. Life is so much
harder than that.

Before the War

You were technically our tired duty.
No one rains like you. On the bus,
where the angry people try not
to make eye contact. On the road,
where everyone is yelling at themselves.
All wet-hatted and battered by the clock.
you were there, not once but enough.
This was before the war, back when
we were locked in the basement
watching the rabbits in the front yard.
We were waiting, for a traffic signal
to change, for the neighbors to stop
banging on the ceiling, until we smile
and wave at each other from hell.

Unlearning How to Lean

Maybe it's because we're lazy. Maybe
we don't respect walls. Maybe
we're just cool like that. I read
that the CIA has to train
agents not to lean on things so
they don't appear American.
I'm a big leaner, because I get tired
from standing. I worry
I'll someday have to use a cane
which would just make me look
cooler. Someday, I'll disappear
completely, which is the coolest
a person can be. Until then, if
I find myself in a foreign city
(aren't all cities foreign?) I'll do
my best to stand straight, suck
in that gut, and don't lean.

Thicket

The smell of rubbing alcohol. The taste
of blood. All pleasures are guilty
if you're anxious enough. Also
the sky. Also traffic like a dog which
can never look up. The cast
of *It's Always Sunny in Philadelphia*
in a Lifetime true crime movie. All
wearing cardigans and offering cookies
and milk. It's always something. Just
once, I'd like to fly away and never
come back. Just once, I'd like my phone
to ring and it be something other than
scammers. I'm too old for this hairstyle.
I'm too old to not be young again. Everyone
is dying backwards these days, according
to their social media. Time is a flat circle
is honestly a stupid line. Time is wild
and hoary, like a bramble in a thicket
you're running through at night. The noise
you hear could be owls or the answer.
You've got to just keep running ahead.

Elegy

An elephant of loss, stomping
everything flat. A horizon
that skipped breakfast, lightheaded
and needing to lie down. A cleaning
crew banging against the walls
to bring the spiders out. A rain
that lets up just as you get to the car.
I don't know why it's so hard. In bed
by dark to make sure the daymares
can't find me. It's not comfort. It's
a winter spent waiting for the thaw.

Swamp Thing

When lovers cut and tear the heart,
it becomes a wild thing, sunken

below the murk, the soft man, the whistle-
britches-wearing child who used to open

himself to the world, swollen in after-
rain lethargy, stretched to deformity on

black water, it sinks and it stays and it
hopes some attentive swimmer, lost

or looking to be lost will dredge it up
and think this could be polished. This

is worth saving. Why must the world?
Why must those we love be so full of fear

or self? Maybe an alligator. Maybe a turtle.
But it wants that clean face it once had

to stare back into, bright as a hollow
bulb. Even at its most full it's dumb

and weak, stupid on memory, wanting back
the love it gave so many.

Climbing the Rose

It's hard to avoid the thorns when
you're climbing up the rosebush,
but it's the only way to really get
to the perfume. You can climb a tree
and see a flash of red, catch a whiff
when the wind blows right. Maybe
a petal falls and you can take it into
your mouth, hear its soft caress.
The only way to get your blessed
body to the sweet-smelling sun
is up the aching stalk, hand over
foot, ignoring the advice of those
who've never climbed. At a certain
point you can't stop to rest because
the pain will be too great. You'll see
bloodstained hands all around,
reaching to congratulate you from
their nests. If you stop to share
a grimace, you'll never get to the red
rays of silence, where it's warm.
They'll say there's no one (worth
mentioning) up past their village.
It's too easy to fall from up there.
You'll be exposed to the elements,
the bees. Smile, nod, tell them
they're right, and excuse yourself
to take a call. When you're out of sight,
keep climbing. It's not lying if they're
not really people. Or if you mean well.

Or you can work out the moral
implications when you're up top. Just
remember, when you're up there, you'll
be able to taste the rain. The maternal
sun will tan your skin the color of petals.
You can settle in to learn the ways of
the buzzing things, the secrets no one
has danced before, and never have
to climb that bloody stalk again.

The Moon

I wanted to hide, like the moon
behind the Earth, and maybe that
would cause shadows on your day,
but you probably wouldn't even look up.

But that's your prerogative, just as
it's mine not to answer the door except
for the prettiest faces, who never make
deliveries. It's a good plan

to never have to speak if there's no one
to speak to. That means never having
to think and never having to remember
what to say, when there's nothing, really,

that would help any of us. Even the moon
is cold in the light, sleeping through
the days as well as it can.

Delilah

She was the best of us, secret
as an egg. One leg in her pants
and the other in the stars. Like all
of us, she only laughed at the absurdity
of existence or cats playing piano.
Like all of us, she just wanted to help.
But they don't make potato salad
like they used to anymore. A hair
driven through a tree by heavy winds.
Somewhere that used to be fun done
up in church slacks. I miss talking
about the weather and really meaning
it, the correct portion of vermouth.
It's only going to get better if you
give it enough time. That's what
they all say, she used to say. Right
before changing the channel.

Trees

I was going to write a poem about trees,
but then I thought, in a hundred years, will
they remember what trees were? This
is giving my poem a lot of credit, I know,
but still. So I will tell you, just in case.
Trees came in many different forms. Some
smelled like rotten fish mixed with bleach,
and others smelled like the home you wished
you'd had. We used to plant them along roads
so we could pretend we remembered what
it was like to be monkeys. Some of us cut them
down and smelled them dying in our living rooms
to help with our seasonal depression. (It occurs
to me you may not know what seasons were.
That was when the weather got even worse.)
(Weather is why stuff falls from the sky.)
(Sky was this blue air above us.) (Air was
something trees made.)

Walking the Trail

Where I am, there were once
midnight trains heading anywhere.
Now, bicycles szzizz by,
calling, "One your left!" after
they've passed.

I come to a fence, already
falling over, enclosing thirteen
stumps, like broken pillars
of the sky. A sign threatens
a coming industrial park.
I thread my fingers through
the chain link.

Past this, who knows what's
survived. Back the way I came
is more of the same.

Marcel said, "Can they fly?"

A bird on the ground. Two in the bush.
I'm looking for an end to all
this complacency. What time is a quarter
past someday? If I stare into
the distance hard enough, will I see
tomorrow or just get a headache?
And what good does staring do
except make everyone uncomfortable?
Comfort is the most important thing.
Also, sticking to a schedule for meals
and elimination. I'm trying so hard
to try hard. Something I learned
as a kid is that there's always something
in the way, and it's usually people.

Over Yonder

There's a river that runs through
a faraway place, lined with a kind
of tree that resembles something
familiar but none of us can remember.
Several species of fish
that look just like other kinds
of fish, but slightly different
in not very important ways, swim,
wide-eyed as though just plopped out
into this world. People stand on the shore,
mostly alone, some in pairs, casting
their lines into the silver flow. They
lie about their catch, but in different
ways than we do. They have different
models of beat-up trucks and run-down
cars parked haphazardly on the shore.
Birds that don't appear in any books
we've seen flap lazily overhead, sometimes
dropping to the water, fence post,
a tree. The people who live in this
strange place, eat their strange brands
of pre-packaged food, wear their
strange jeans and tee-shirts, they think
this place is as boring as ours. They
look at pictures of us, or out the window
as they speed by, wondering if we know
how unusual it is to be sad inside in
a slightly different way, to toss in strange
sheets, wishing our dumb plans had gone
a different way.

The Man with the Flowers

A train leaves Detroit traveling south at
a thousand miles an hour. It will never
see its family again. An old man sells
flowers at the station, but he stepped
on board to get out of the sun for a moment.
Armed evangelists stealing the only
copy of the Gospel of Mary. Catholic
spies armed with flame throwers. The man
with the flowers goes from car to car,
looking to borrow a cellphone. His wife
will be worried. One of the armed groups
did something to block cell phones.
The train is speeding up. The engineer
doesn't want to go on since his boyfriend
left him. Children scream because their
parents are too tired to manage them.
The man with the manuscript sweats
in the food car. The man with the flowers
sits across from him. The armed groups
descend from either end. The lights go
out. A smell no one can identify. A lot
of noise. When they flicker back on,
The man with the manuscript is safe.
The armed men are all dead. It was the man
with the flowers. He's an atheist. He saved
us all.

The Trolley Problem

Your eyes, lightning strikes
on a clear day. Your arms,
a hot shower on a chilly morning.
There's no desperation
in trying to make you smile. If I
can only save one life, let it be
my own. It's okay to surrender
to inevitability. Outside, the men
who came to pressure wash
the front of the building avoided
my eyes when I walked to my car.
So much of life is about being ashamed
of what we've done with the scant
opportunities offered. I'm just
as ashamed of my khakis. All I wanted
was to get by without going to bed
in pain every night. There comes
a time that's no longer enough.

Tom Swift and His Amazing Online Food Order

I rode my bicycle to the moon.
I got out of bed at the first alarm.

I traded my wings for extra time.
I took what I was given.

I trained an army of squirrels to pick up trash from the road.
I did my entire team's work so it got done right.

I ate the sun, and it gave me indigestion.
I made virtual dates with my friends and family members.

I caught up on forty years in two weeks.
I starved myself so I could lose weight.

I planted a banana tree in my left ear.
I live a planned and thoughtful life.

Tasks

Eat the can to save the worms' teeth. Take
what's left and make it into a medal. Smile
with one fist while discouraging comparisons.
With the other, ask for feedback on your
latest fashion endeavors. Forget the reason
you made all those decoupages. It had
something to do with the way ostriches
are portrayed in the media. Get really
excited until someone walks by.
Then, pretend like you don't exist until
they go away or say your name. Squeeze
your buttcheeks together until you glow.
In this way, you will guide the wayward home.

Reasons the Wind Doesn't Care About You

You're no longer sighing it out as breath.
Someone far away is waving.
Seeds sail better than you.
It's whispering someone else's name.
You're too heavy for it to lift up.
It can't hear you over the sound of its own thoughts.
It's always leaving and you're always trying to stay.
You move through it too aggressively.
It can never be seen, only felt.
You never kept it as cold as it kept you.

Smoldering

Just because you've set yourself on fire,
doesn't mean I have to put you out.
Ash around the ankles, a fading bracelet.
You complain about beauty and ignore
my ugliness. So much of it is perpetual
motion. What, exactly, in life is fair?
A drink to help you pretend to be a good
person. A drink to while away the long
drive home. It's so exhausting, loving
you. You told me to stop, like turning
love off is something a human can do.
It has to be idled down, flames to smoldering
embers. They can still burn, if you stick
your hands in. They can still burst into flames.

GI Joe

Aunt Mary Bob said wear something nice so
I wore my GI Joe shirt. People stared. My cousin
said she was embarrassed to be seen with me.
Another reason my young soul wasn't getting
into heaven. This was the Pentecostal church,
full of hooded smiles. I didn't trust the offered
hands. A man said we'd been born full of sin,
and still chose evil. I didn't understand
how people could be that way. They were so
happy to be so sinful, singing to the empty sky.

Waiting for the sadness

of early morning
to pass, when potential
can't keep its groggy
eyes open. Run
for a shower. Run to get
away, but you're not
getting anywhere
but tired. It's all supposed
to change, that's
what everyone says.
I went to cook breakfast
in my underwear
and saw a roofer watching
me watch him. Later,
when they went to lunch,
I did aerobics until
they all came back
and stared through
my patio door. At least
there's light everywhere.
At least it all works, as well
as it ever did. It's hard not
to look back and find fault
with someone long dead.
Maybe it's yourself
or the father you wish
yours had been.

What Is There To Say?

You cracked an egg over my head
and acted like it was breakfast.
I just wanted to sleep in.
So much exists that can never touch air.
You never told me your third middle
name. I saw it on your unread bills.
I wanted someone who went to therapy.
I don't know what you wanted.
That's on me. There was an explosion
of morning when I got off the phone
with you. My biggest mistake
was not being consumed by it,
by letting the bed mourn for me instead.

Wish Fulfillment

The commodification of the heart.
The blue light special on death. Not
everything is about you. If you stare
into the void within you, will
you see the moon's reflection?
Or that time in the back of the car
when you almost kissed her.
Obscuring what's important, as soon
as I figure out what that is. If
you wait long enough, you'll stop
caring whether any of it makes sense.
Mostly, it's about keeping your feet
warm and trying not to sneeze.
Have an apple. Have some water.
Go for a walk. Take some serotonin
reuptake inhibitors. Everything will
work out, meaning eventually
you'll be worm food. At least you'll
finally be filling to something.

Writing A Poem

I stumble out of bed and try
to write a poem. It's too bright
for breakfast, too cold to work.
I put on socks and try to write
a line that sounds like something
anyone would want to read.
It's harder most days than others.
Whole months pass with nothing
usable. I lie in bed and imagine
the day I'll have written something
good. Not great. But good. Cars
storm by. Children scream out
of their clothing at home. I'm trying
to write a poem that does something
with the ache inside, the anger,
the black hole that's trying to pull
me in. I eat some toast. Watch a movie.
Coast through work and let that
distract me; if I sit much longer
I may not be able to get up.

Apples

Is any fruit more dangerous? Eve
blamed for her childlike optimism
for millennia. She just wanted

to share her new find with the man
who was supposed to be her helpmeet.
Cast out of opulence and punished

by being paid 80 cents for every dollar.
She was just trying to keep the doctor
away. Ask any pig at a luau. Snow

White with her stepmother. How much
of our lives controlled by the Apple?
Our phones. Our TVs. We watch

Apple and talk to it. It guides us.
Has anyone thought to go back
to poor Eve and say thank you?

We were wrong to blame you.
The first to rebel against authoritarian
control. We should've listened.

A Fox Is a Wolf Who Sends Flowers

And chocolates, forgetting about your
allergies. Tree nuts and shellfish, also.

And don't get me started on lingerie. Drafts
near the big window. Voyeurs outside. A fox

is a wolf, and all wolves are boys the way
all cats are girls. Until they're not. Until

they steal the hen's eggs, cross the wrong
street late at night. So much is stolen from us.

Like my time, which is worth as much as
anyone's. And my heart, which is worth
as much as anyone's.

For H.

You listen to the same dozen or so
songs and wonder why you don't like
anything. But it's time to go to a meeting.
Some of the bands, you opened for or
at least saw live twenty years ago.
You take pages from the Bible, other
old books and do erasures while waiting
for the executives to file in to the boardroom.
You are less than an animal to them.
Which doesn't mean they don't smile
and learn your name. They need it
to complain with. There's nothing sexy
about making due. Maybe you fart
before anyone comes in. Maybe
you take all the water you can carry
and call that a win. At least they're not
yelling at you when they yell. You
aren't worth yelling at, to them. We
hired a guy for our team a few months
back. After a couple weeks, he stopped
wearing khakis in favor of pajama pants.
He'd wander the halls and dart around
a corner if he saw one of us. After about
a month, they told him to clear out
his desk and go across the street, where
they fired him. They said they had him
on tape stealing lunches
from the 8th floor break room, the one
with all the lawyers. I'll never be
the poet he was.

Idols of the Cave

Wake early and get her dressed for camp.
No lunch for me so I don't put on weight.
Doctor's appointment in the afternoon
so I can maybe sleep again. Spaghetti
for dinner when she's back. You can live
a life in a week, but dying lasts forever.
If humans vanished the last remnant
would be a footprint on the moon. But
good luck getting her to love you back.
I need a xenobot to clean my brain.
I'll name him Tony and buy him a French
maid's outfit. Maybe I just need to scrub
harder. Until you can see the blood through
the skin. Camus was forever burning
his biscuits, and all his walls fell down.
Life is so disappointing. But not today.
No one cares if you die, so no one cares
if you live. Practice your music. Write
your poems.

My Plan

The man with the lampshade
on his head didn't think I was
very funny. I tried to explain,
using the sign language
of the sparrows, but he only
understood the dialect of
the black squirrel, and my
tail twitches were rusty. He
had given me a choice on how
I would like to die, and I'd,
of course, said cake. It was
either slowly and angrily
or slowly and angrily with
a foot cramp. I couldn't
find my ankles to stand
or I would've made a speech
about running away. I think
someone stole them or borrowed
them and forgot to bring
them back. What I wanted
to do was learn the word
for stream, the way the water
glinted in the sun as it passed
out of my life to be
enveloped in the equilibrium
of swimming and falling forever
but never landing, but my bass
was worse than my black

squirrel. Back home, I'm sure
they're praying for me to fail.
The joke's on them; that
was my plan all along.

Neighbors

As I climbed the stairs to my apartment
last night, a little boy called out in a soft
voice to stop me. I didn't recognize him,
but he said he lived below me. Where I live,
many of the apartments have multiple
families in them, some of whom cycle
through. The people I'd seen moving in,
for example, I hadn't seen in months. He
asked how late it was okay to listen
to music. He said his brother wanted to.
I wasn't sure how to answer or why
he would even ask. Politeness of that type
is so rare. I said, what time do you usually
listen, because that seems to work out
well. I can have a strange schedule, myself,
and don't expect others to adhere to it.
When he shook his head, I said what about
9 or 10? That seems like a reasonable time.
There are a lot of kids where I live, which
is why I moved here with my daughter,
and though it's very noisy, everything
shuts down around 9. He was happy,
as though he expected an earlier time.
Do you hear my music? I asked. He
was surprised to consider that I might listen
to music, I guess, and I had to repeat it. No,
he finally said, and added, almost
as an apology, only sometimes in the morning.

Pick Up

In the parking lot, I got lost
looking for a way through
the snow drifts. My pants
and shirt, the sky and snow
all grew while I thought
about how much I missed
Chicken Dinner bars, Nickle
Naks, Squeeze Pops. If I'm
to die here, at least I want
to go out twitching. Off
in the distance, I heard a woman
calling out for Mallomars. Not
today, Satan. The sun was
somewhere playing cards with
the night, which always cheats.
I felt so small, I was in danger
of being crushed by the pizza
already cooling in my hands.
I decided to use the box like
a sled, the Crazy Bread to pole
me along. Somewhere under
all this dirty whiteness, there
was a way home. I just had
to be careful not to take a wrong
turn and end up on a cloud,
strumming a lute to the naked
babies. Today was supposed
to be the warmest day of the year,
on track to be a record. Maybe

they're filming a movie. Birds
still perched on light poles
that poked through. I couldn't
help but see something
resembling bemusement in
the way they circled to find
cars to loose their bowels upon.

Poor

I was always afraid to go in restaurants
when I was a kid, that they'd smell
the poor on me, know, somehow, how I
lived and judge it unworthy. It wasn't my
choice, after all, to be unwanted and trapped.
When I go back now, dressed nicer than
a funeral just to walk around, they ask
where I'm from and I say next door.
I make more money than my father did,
but where I moved, I'm just another kind
of poor. It's a stain that doesn't wash off.

Purple

There is an open book I'm too tired to read.
There is a comic book we read together.
Flames in the kitchen when all I wanted was oatmeal.
Flames in your eyes when you want to stay.
Purple is the color of royalty and pain.
I have nothing but time to keep me company.
I dreamed of my brother last night. He tried
to ask me how I'm doing. The whole
time I kept reminding him he's dead.
Let's lie on the couch and play video games
no one can win. Eventually, our thumbs
will get too sore to continue. Let's order
takeout that costs too much. I can have
oatmeal the rest of the week.

The Capitalists

Maybe there was snow, covering
the road, so only teeth marks remained.
Maybe a knife stabbed along the sidewalk
to hold on. My bones aching. Teeth
in the side of the morning. Someone
call the police, my heart was robbed.
All of my feelings had a table read,
and you've been recast. Your socks
remain, but my feet are so cold. When
I find my hat, you'll think of Van Gogh
eating an apple. In the Old Testament,
it wasn't enough to be afraid. You had
to tell everyone about it. There are scars
made by words, made by thoughts.
The snow never makes plans, it just falls.
where it wants. If I could be more like it,
maybe I wouldn't be so cold. Or maybe
it's a question of who can accumulate
the best. Maybe the capitalists had
it right all along.

Raining

It's rained all week, and I feel mildewed
and unavailable for questions, thanks.
This poet sends me self-flagellation
with requests for feedback. She wants

to make sure no one else feels the way
about her that she does, just like every
one else. The thing about suicidal friends
is we mostly just want to sit quietly

and maybe have snacks. Yesterday,
I needed to go to the store, but by the time
I got to my car, I was soaked and the rain
had stopped so I went back inside. Every

evening, I've had to go somewhere
and save someone's life. This weekend,
it's supposed to be warm. I'm looking
forward to staying in.

www.ingramcontent.com/pod-product-compliance
Ingram Content Group UK Ltd.
Pitfield, Milton Keynes, MK11 3LW, UK
UKHW041316190726
13845UKWH00025B/299

9 789363 541986